Two great sensibilities play out in these gorgeous, hard-hitting poems: American Transcendentalism and Literary Modernism. Kann's unique synthesis of style and sensibility is a revelation. There is a heartfelt confession unfolding here—accumulating in a variety of forms and styles—held together by a rare and authentic voice of profound emotional honesty.

R.L. Inchausti, Ph.D.

Rage and reconciliation braid themselves through these poems that chronicle the speaker's emergence from suppressed memories of abuse and parental obfuscation, intertwining them with the brutality and powerful obsessiveness he finds in the characters in a discarded copy of *Moby Dick* while working summers as a city-bred teenager on a Berkshires farm. In its pages, he finds mirrors of his own half-grasped anguish; but too, in farm life he finds consolation in the lessons of the natural world. With a lushness akin to Melville's in its forceful metaphor and eloquent descriptions, Kann interweaves buried memories, swatches from Melville himself, and scenes of an agrarian world where brutality is sometimes necessary but never deceptive or ill-intended, and where peace also can be found.

Leslie Ullman,
author of *Little Soul and the Selves*

I've always been drawn to the fire in David Kann's work—fierce, hungry, and beautifully contained. *Ishmael on the Farm* operates across a sweeping emotional and physical landscape, ranging from silenced childhood trauma in New York City through teenage summers on a Berkshire farm, from the pages of *Moby Dick* to the redemptive power of language and writing. Here are poems that are shaped by physical labor ("simple / as cleaning a slaughterhouse with a steam hose"), that do not look away from sorrow ("Home was a closed fist / clenched around a wail") and that exist in ecstatic connection to the living world ("peepers sing like spun foil in the dark," "the smell of struck flint that comes before snow"). This is a remarkable book.

Lisa Coffman,
author of *Likely* and *Less Obvious Gods*

Ishmael on the Farm

by David Kann

Fernwood
PRESS

Ishmael on the Farm

©2024 by David Kann

Fernwood Press
Newberg, Oregon
www.fernwoodpress.com

Printed in the United States of America

Cover and page design: Mareesa Fawver Moss
Cover photo: Ansgar Scheffold
Author photo: Lois Kann

ISBN 978-1-59498-126-5

Gratefully dedicated to Lois, my wife and partner;
Rachel, Jennifer, Benn, and Arielle, the best of us;
and also to my teachers: Jody Gladding, Matthew Dickman, and Leslie Ullman;
and finally to Lisa Coffman, who knows why.

Contents

Acknowledgment

In 2015, my chapbook *The Language of the Farm* was published by Five Oaks Press. It was based on my experiences on the Shaker Village Work Group's farm. In 2019, my chapbook *Blues for Pip* was published by Finishing Line Press. It was based on my late-arriving knowledge of my molestation and coming to terms with it. Only after these two works were published did I see how they defined each other and my experience. I've chosen poems from each book, combined them, revised them extensively, and added a substantial number of new poems to make this book.

Introduction

At some point between the ages of two and three I was sexually molested by a caregiver. This I learned through a combination of flashes of memory and conversations with a friend, a psychologist, regarding the behavior of men who have been molested as children (Thanks, Matt!), allowing me to correlate my past behavior, fantasies, and thoughts with the event and to reverse engineer myself to the understanding of what had happened to me and of my subsequent actions.

My parents must have known or at least suspected, but they never mentioned the matter to me, the conspiracy of silence and shame over such matters being common in their generation. By the time I had come to this knowledge in my sixties, they were dead, which is to say this is all speculation. But it makes sense to me.

It also makes sense to me that the series of molestations and the subsequent silence taught me that trust is valuable currency and that to invest it in those figures purported to be sources of love, comfort, and security may be a dangerous venture. Further, whether the molestation was painful or pleasurable, it elicited sensations for which my child-self was unprepared. They were terrifying, which brings me to *Moby Dick* and Ishmael, Ahab, and ultimately Pip.

I've taught *Moby Dick* many times, but one class stands out. There were three reentry students, all mothers of young children. They immediately understood Ahab and Ishmael as lost children wounded by a world that had disappointed their expectations of comfort, protection, parental love, benevolent nurture, justice, and security. By extension, Ahab's "Anacharsis Cloots deputation" of a crew were all abandoned children dealing in different ways with their rage and pain. (For example, Stubb, the second mate. "I've been thinking over it ever since, and that ha, ha's the final consequence. Why so? Because a laugh's the wisest, easiest answer to all that's queer.") Out of their agony they submitted to Ahab, their wounded avatar, and to his quest to discover, defeat—or in his absence create in himself—God-the-father by destroying God-incarnate, the leviathan that had wounded him.

I spent my fourteenth through seventeenth summers at the Shaker Village Work Group in New Lebanon, New York. Almost from the moment I arrived there, I was drawn to the farm. The brutal, beautiful, sensible nature of the place, the logic of the work shaped by the essential rhythms of the seasons made sense to me, so different from the tissue of lies and evasions at home. All the matters of birth and death, sowing and harvesting, fallow and fertile were reflected in language that cut away anything that obscured or was extraneous to the moment, its consequences, and the job to be done. If language really does create and change one's perceptions, I began to learn to see through evasions and the nuances of civilized expression (Melville: "snivilization") to get at the necessities organic to the round of days and seasons. I learned to give myself to that exacting, nurturing world and to open myself to it, letting it embrace me and fill me. As it opened to me, so I filled it. Like Ishmael, I learned that living is a matter of balance between opposites, like a river and its banks, letting each one shape and fill the other and thereby become each other.

The three skeins: the farm's shaping, healing power; my subsequent reading and rereading and teaching *Moby Dick*; and my late-in-life discovery of my molestation and the realization that I had been chasing the phantom of that sad, sick person for most of my life, braided then culminated in this collection of poems.

There may be wisdom—terrifying, pleasurable, or both—that we're offered too soon, child or adult: a Black cabin boy on a nineteenth-century whaler; the captain of a whaler forced to cope with undeserved harm; the able seaman who served on his crew; a twentieth-century fortunate child secure in his warm bed facing thrilling, seductive terror. Or perhaps it's forced on us, leaving speaking scars that beg silently in the night for us to embrace our truths and tell them.

All of this,
being only words,
may not surrender
or surround
the truth.
Yet it's all the truth I know
and all the language I've got,
leaving me comforted
by naming

Fetus in Fetu

Coiled brother
who wears
my blood
my bones
my skin's
desire
who whispers
my rage
in our secret ear
who takes
my breath my breath
for his
who takes
my voice my voice
for his
who takes
my dreams my dreams
for his
terrified rage
that drives us
when I feel
his fists
against my heart
inside
my heart's beat
doubled
his teeth gnaw
my guts

That Central Moment

when desire looked like love
and wore a nanny's white dress,
when her wide, white eyes nailed me
where I lay,
three years old and bedtime-drowsy,
tucked tight in bright white sheets.
The room was drenched in steam heat's musk;
winter's pale wind rattled the window in its sash,
and sleet tapped at the glass like bone fingers.
She stood in a lamp's slant light.
She snagged me with her desperate eyes
while her fingers slow-danced down her buttons.
Her bright white dress parted and clotted at her bare feet.
She bent forward with her hair hanging over her face,
did some sleight of hand behind her back,
and her breasts fell free, tapered at the top,
then round and full, swaying, swelling,
and glowing like moons in the dim room
but for their brown, shadowed nipples.
She hooked her thumbs in the elastic denting her waist.
Then she was naked.
I couldn't look away
from that mat of dark hair
and that dreadful absence.
She walked toward me, stirring the air
with the odors of lavender and yeast.
A mystery of slow, thick flame rose in my groin.
I couldn't take it in.
I couldn't take it.
I couldn't take
my eyes away
as she slid her hand into that wiry tangle,
as she rocked and rocked against her fingers and palm,

gasped, her stomach suddenly tight-ridged.
I drowned in the alien pleasure that poured from her
    other hand;
I brimmed with a blaze too huge to contain.
Suddenly I was all flame.
Then she
left,
left me,
left me here,
still searching for that moment,
to restore that white-fired revelation
and escape the following plummet
that first leaves me calm,
then leaves me
with mindless, ravenous monkey-lust
hooting and howling in my flesh,
leading me,
leaving me,
lost.

Isn't there any bandage, suture, salve or balm
to soothe this gnawing or close this wound,
that cries betrayal, rage,
ecstatic terror and terrified ecstasy,
tangled dread and desire,
so snarled it will not unknot itself,
so every caress contains a curse
and every hug holds a howl?

All this, being only words,
may not surrender
or surround
the truth,
yet it is all the truth I know
and all the language I've got,
leaving me comforted
by naming,
believing myself whole-
ly safe and total-
ly (self) aware—
with my 20/20 sight and seismic sensitivity
to another's slightest tic or tremor;
a pupil's dilation,
the tilt of a head,
the slightest smile,
a warm palm's curl and cup,
the press of fingertips against my back,
the sight and scent of a body
rocking with quickening breath,
eyes liquid and dark—
not knowing that my eyes and ears,
fogged by loss and deafened
by nighttime's pitiless yammer,
don't get that consummation's long gone
beyond my reach and rage.

Secrets

Home was a closed fist
clenched around a wail,
nails dug into a palm,
gouging red gashes in my flesh
silence that conspired
to strangle the real agony
I could never speak
into all that tense hush
that stifled history,
deflected wounding truths

where what words there were
wove a careful course
between pits and snares
placation, compromise, equivocation:
no more than noise to drown
the endless hum of rage
droning under the voices;

words heaped like an earth dam
growing more saturated with evasion,
just endless phony phrases,
repeated day by day:
spackle for the pits and cracks
in fear's frail and flimsy wall,
rebuilt over and over—

no more than words, no more
than crumbs that fall
from bread turned to stone:
the petrified loaf of the world
crumbled to scattered scraps,
each truth pinioned, axon by dendrite,
into a mesh of nodes and nerves,
a gossamer scrim,
a spiderweb scam,
a lying cosmetic,
a steel-cable net
heaved at a beast too huge to bind,
first sieving dark oceans, wavering
then pursed, drawn inward and close,
hauling deep-sea life to the surface
to gasp, convulse, and die.

Still, true words may voice a vision.
A voice may shape a world.
A world may change a mind.
A mind may sing a new song.

The Language of the Farm

makes no promises but speaks
of facts without frill or filigree,
free of compromise and doubt
plumb and solid as well-sunk fenceposts,
bordering the fields
where the spring's canons and fugues
rise from new-harrowed fields,
that fill the air
with the lush, dark smell of turned loam
ready to be plowed into furrows' long reach.
Pale green stems spread their first leaves,
and wind strews blossoms' feathery consequence.
Summer's midday Sabbath silence
reveals the crackle of growing corn
and the contented grunts of nursing sows
sprawled on their sides
and cows' patient breath
where they stand and graze
before the cadences of afternoon.
Coming harvest's dark hum's hints
fill August's thick air that blurs the trees around the fields;
Then, the smell of haying rises like spring's second bloom
from cut stalks ready to be raked into straight lines
across autumn's stubbled fields
strewn with bright leaves' farewell confetti.
Fall's coming cold brings slaughter's
and blood's necessary stipulations
speaking the inconsequence of any single life
and the consequence of the pigs' daily slop.

Then the smell of struck flint that comes just before snow,
rides on wind so bitter we're driven behind wooden walls
to rest secure in long nights' silences
lit by maple, oak, and birch logs' flames
laid by against the early dark and rising cold
where we sleep the earth's winter sleep,
dreaming in the farm's pure words,
secure in our beds,
warm in the sweet smell of hay drifting from the hayloft
when the winter moon pours tarnished silver over the land.

Reading *Moby Dick* on the Farm, 1

Whenever I find myself growing grim about the mouth, and bringing;
whenever it is a damp, drizzly November in my soul; whenever I find myself
involuntarily pausing before coffin warehouses, and bringing up the rear
of every funeral procession I meet; and especially when my hypos get such
an upper hand of me that it requires a strong moral principle to prevent
me from deliberately stepping into the street, and methodically knocking
people's hats off—then I account it high time to get to sea as soon as I can.

Free of necessary routines of a Sunday,
I rummaged in the dark in a box in the back of the barn.
I found this book, water-stained, smelling of blood and salt.
Ishmael's desperate rage
against snivilization's compromises pulled me in,
and I've read it over the summer weeks
in free times syncopated against chores' tempo.

Now, I sit here, by the still pond
where the woods almost reach the shore,
sunk in its smell of water, algae, and spawning fish,
my back against a pine, in its cool shade,
adrift in harvest smells
among the uncanny Berkshires,
where he wrote this hell-fired book,
secure under Greylock's sheltering brow,
only a few miles from Nathaniel:
his secret brother, father, and more secret love,
Nathaniel's shyness gnawed at his heart
that longed and loved him past loving.
Nathaniel's puzzled, careful affection, perplexed
at his god-estranged, restless search
for a ground of belief, or unbelief,
raising a wall between them,
both driven by memory's white fire
that burned belief to lonely rage

and words to empty gestures—
the lost hope of a place
free of denial and deception,
sharing his father-loss of home,
disinherited of scripture's certainty.

But now the hayfield's gold flickers between the trees
and a breeze bears the sweet smell of hay drying on haymows
where I sit, bound over to this book,
its pages rippling like the hem of a white dress.
Here I sit, within shouting distance of Arrowhead,
far inland from where he had launched himself
from freezing Nantucket, wondering how—
in the midst of these mountains
whose certain change each year from light green
to a green deep as dreaming,
to autumn's mortal confetti-strew,
to the terrible monochrome of winter
and back to blossom, bloom, and blow—
he could imagine the inconstant sea,
Ishmael's rage and all the terrors of the deep
in that room where he sat, writing all day
until Elizabeth's no-nonsense knock roused him to dinner
and the daily comfort of feeding the horses and cow:
a safe harbor after sailing into his storm,
self-given to its gales and currents,
rogue waves hurling him between belief and disbelief,
willing to risk broaching broadside to them,
turning turtle and sinking without a trace
while the sea rolled on, unmoved
as it has since the cosmos blasted into being
or since god's hand reached down
to stroke the firmament, soil and sea to life,

accountable only to himself for its terrors—
leviathan and storm, tsunami and temblor.

But there is comfort
in the green, surrounding mountains
and their reflection in this mirroring pond,
and the smell of hot pine needles, cut hay,
still water, mud, frogs and fish, bark and balsam.
How necessary the benign Berkshires must have seemed
and how necessary to cleave to Nathaniel,
to dedicate this hell-fired book to him,
who had learned how to sail on a steady heading
no matter how turbulent the gale-churned sea,
his poise like ballast in that raging storm.
He knew the cost of Nathaniel's serenity,
like holy oil spread on the ocean,
calming the tempest that followed Jonah,
swallowed into hell's belly
to learn where power lies.
He saw Nathaniel and himself—
brothers in knowing the weight
of bearing blackness ten times black,
secretly crying *No!* in thunder,
knowing all those who say *yes*, lie;
and all those who say *no* live unencumbered
carrying no more baggage
than their reality-creating selves.

Here I sit, leaning against the irrefutable trunk of this pine
with this book that with every word
asks me how I came to be here
to learn the farm's factual, cyclic language
that strips away illusion and so affirms,
calms, consoles, and contains the submerged life,
eases it into the mind's sight
to speak with clearer words
in the farm's stricter tongue,
brother to this book,
that offers a squeeze of the hand
and the call to walk together,
looking neither forward
to the unforseen turns
nor back to all those daydreams of explanation.

Death of Innocents

We were fourteen- and fifteen-year-old
wise-ass city kids who knew a lot about sidewalks,
tenements, stoops, subways, busses
and how to navigate streets-in-a-grid,
bussed from New York's summer swelter
to live and work on an upstate farm.

Still groggy from being awakened early
and confused by the dirt road's meander
and the ragged borders of woods and fields,
we stared around, strangers to each other,
trying to bridge the gulfs with bits of sentences,
silently judging each other's clothes, shoes, hair,
trapped in our angular, tender bodies.

We were bunched behind a swaybacked barn.
On one side there was a fresh trench
under two poles joined by a board
that seemed to grow splinters while I watched,
with four broad, dented zinc funnels nailed to it.
On the other side, a deep-bellied black pot
simmered scummy water over a low fire.
Next to the pot, a door on sawhorses
marbled with raised black stains like blood-blisters.

And then there were
low wooden cages with dowel-bars,
stacked three high, three across
with chickens crammed
into a heaving, shit-stained, feathered mass.
Amber eyes looked through the bars
where quiet clucking and crooning rose.

A farmhand walked up and told us to watch him.
He yanked a bird by the neck
through a door at the top of a cage,
flipped it and grabbed it by its legs.
It squawked, flapped and shed feathers
until he shoved it head-first
into one of the funnels,
drew its head through.
A knife appeared in his other hand.
Then, with a casual left-right slash
he cut the bird's throat.
The loose head dangled,
and there was a soft patter into the trench.
My breath stopped.
The trees' rustle stopped.
I believe the clouds stopped.

Some of us were sent to the cages,
given small knives with wooden handles
and burred crosshatching on the blades.
I drew a chicken out by its head
and grabbed it by its scaly legs.
It jerked my arm around,
upside-down, neck curved upward,
scrawing, wings flapping, shedding feathers
until I jammed it into a funnel.
I reached in for its wedge head—
like pinching my heart.
It fought against my fingers,
tried to pull back.
Then I yanked it through.
One blinking amber eye nailed me.

I drew back and left the chicken there,
wings pinned, scaly yellow talons grabbing at the sky
under the early summer sun's slant dapple.
The head jerked left and right,
the beak opening and closing,
chewing the air.

I took a deep breath.
With the knife in one hand,
the head held in the other,
I slashed.
Too deep.
The head dropped into my palm.
Blood poured through my fingers,
down my forearm, dripped from my elbow.
I flung the head in the trench.
The eyes were still rolling,
the beak searching for breath to cry out.
Spinning about, wringing and shaking my hands,
I sent bird blood flying everywhere,
staining my face and my new white T-shirt.
Everything stopped.
Everyone stared at me.

What else could I do under their gaze
but take another bird?
Then three other kids joined in.
Together, it seemed easier.
We grabbed, stuffed and slashed,
grabbed, stuffed and slashed.
We passed the drained birds, heads dangling,
combs gone pale pink, to the black scalding pot,
then to the feather-plucking machine's rolling beaters

and then to the next table
where they were butchered.
We split the naked, pale-yellow bodies down the belly,
sorted through ropes of intestine and green gall bladders,
for red gizzards, garnet-lobed livers.
The air was filled with slither and slop.
The barn cats under the table
yowled and clawed over spilled innards.

I'd always wondered if the expression was true.
I found a dull, rusted, split-shanked, hand-axe,
took a chicken,
stretched it out on a stump,
struck at its neck, two times, three times,
until the head flew to the side.
The bird body sprang out of my hand,
running and tumbling in blind somersaults,
blood spurting from its crushed neck
that spasmed in and out of its feathered stump.
All of us were crimson-splattered.

First, we stared.
Then we laughed.
Then we roared,
then howled,
then danced around the twitching white rag of the dead bird
and the blood-muddy killing trench.
We smeared each other's faces with chicken blood,
heaved guts at each other
until we were speckled with flecks of liver,
draped with thin blue strings of intestine,
painted with shit.

That night,
I lay with a girl,
feeling the consequence of murder
in my blooded hands
against her living warmth
stretched beside me.
And I rose
with the moon into the night.
I rose,
loving death and our flesh,
I rose
into the brawling dark
with all its spinning stars,
over pines' flickering black flames
trembling with crickets' ratchet
and nighthawks' bright calls.

And when we came,
we spoke the wordless
language of pure sound
not with consonants
that chopped moments
into manageable pieces
but with moans
that stretched time,
that wove us into the night
with our braided voices
speaking our ecstasy
with our vowels' canticle
under the moon-shadowed Berkshires.

One Night in the Berkshires

That night the moon stroked the pond with silver
until it quivered with such desire
its underwater weeds writhed and twisted
and caressed the fish so they moaned with lust.
They dreamed in the wet dark
of swapping fins for arms and hands
to touch, caress, and hold, palms cupped full
and for legs to tangle and twine,
and to trade scales for smooth skin
rosy with warm blood rising,
delighting in lips and tongues.
Their longing drove the pond
to leap from its bed,
rise toward the sky
and sing a hankering hallelujah across the land.
So, the hills fell to their knees,
bowed their stone heads,
worshiping flesh-dreams with a sad hoorah
that split the green ground open,
and at the sight, pale clouds woke from their slow drift,
rushed into ashy heaps
and poured down with a choral roar.

Call Me Ishmael

His hand will be against every man, and every man's hand against him.

1.

Call me Ishmael, raging:
lost child searching for home:
Ish—the sound of ice-clogged winter waves against an oak hull
May—choices yet unmade, clutter and chaos awaiting a
    shaping touch
Ell—an unexpected turn in the road, the hidden curve.
Not my name, but the word that speaks me.

2.

Drawn down to Sunday New York harbor, one in a crowd
lost in a leafless forest of masts, spars, and bowsprits
clmbing vines of rigging, shrouds, and ratlines
part of a mob loomed over by figureheads—
a sea-angel with a lantern to light the way
a blue-tailed mermaid's seduction of the sea
an armed and shielded warrior defying the waves.
I'm adrift, knowing the risks better
than the blank-eyed, suicidal Sunday crowd,
drawn from stone churches,
where they sat tucked securely in their pews,
tarnished under the color of stained-glass fables,
now entranced to the edge of the land, where it ends.
Even here, close-harbored among piers and pilings
that mute and buffer the waves' slosh,
they come from their worship
to stare into the great blank of the sea,
turned from their weekday world
where they're nailed to desks and documents.
Which, then, is the truer worship?

3.

It's the thrill of secret knowledge
that draws them to knowing beyond
what they've been told to know,
now staring hopefully, frightfully
into the white void of sea and sky,
looking for the breach and spout.
It's not the choking purse-net of scripture
that knots my back and clenches my fist.
It's desire that keeps me in the game,
questioning blue heaven's cloudless blank
or water's surface-glare
reflecting the sky in reciprocal camouflage,
and an instant's touch and smell
on a winter night in a shared bed
spent curled together, belly to butt.

4.

Restless and remembering that moment,
I walk down a winter road bending seaward,
eye-stung, with the taste of salt and stone on my lips.
Gale-flailed beach grass, blown and bent,
thrashes under sheets of sand.
The road becomes a high-crowned rut
leading to a prairie-flat headland slanting to the surf.
The wind drives clots of white and tan foam
to tangle in a rockweed high-tide line.
The ocean is sun and spume-striped,
gale-blurred, blank and bright,
hiding its eely, savage life under its mirroring blue,
reminding me that as the vacant eyes
of the ocean stare down the shore

while its jaws gnaw the land to pieces,
so in me there lies one insular atoll,
a reef cupping a calm lagoon
surrounded by all the fanged horrors of my lizard-life.

5.

If I were sure of the Great Charlatan's hoax,
I might have disappeared landward into the brawling night
to grope my way back
to vision bounded by forest and hills;
not this terrifying horizon
but sturdy walls, hearthstone and mantel,
warm suppers, warm blankets, and friends;
a wife, who lived in my heart,
our bed, table and fireside,
where I might speak my own name
and live in all that's kind to our mortalities.

6.

Call me Ishmael:
name for my rage,
my longing to know,
my search for home,
undone by hunger that reaches back
to Ahab, my wounded captain,
my aggrieved father, my forbearer, myself,
avatar of us all,
who sails before me still.
Ishmael: contingent word for me, survivor,
the only one returned to tell thee,
myself left raging, unraveled, and dispossessed.

Frenzy

College was distant from my family and its silences,
the clouds of denial and trivia. I could finally see

where I could barely bring myself to look,
and the sight peeled me to my nerves, raw, and raging.

Some stormy winter mornings I woke in the hooting dark,
each radiator clank a hammer to my heart,

sweating and soaked, with flame rising in my gut.
I'd clamp my lips and clench my teeth

against recalled words speaking dreams
that terrified and shamed me.

I'd pull on sweatpants and a T-shirt and sneakers
and let myself out into the storm's gray twilight.

Blowing snow blurred the trees and filled the road;
each tree trunk was honed with white.

The cold and wind were a comfort to my heat—
like the assurance of a heavy quilt at night.

In the back of the building, behind a brick wall
was a dumpster and a bin filled with bottles.

I gathered some bottles and lined them up on the wall
Fanta Fanta Fanta Fanta Fanta Fanta.

I chucked rocks I took from a pile of leftover gravel
soothed by the slide and play of muscle and stone's solid heft.

Each bottle blossomed with silvery shards of glory.
Each crash sounded somehow like a sigh,

like a sigh . . . like her sigh . . . like my sigh
into sleep as that fire was banked for a time.

Winter's Rage

The pond speaks winter in late afternoon's reflected light
under sooty clouds dragging dark from the east.
Sunset's no more than a lighter stain against the west's
    steely ceiling.
There's no ripple, no stir of wind.
Bare willow branches barely score the surface,
no fish-dimples where they'd snatched a drowning bug.
Ice fangs the banks and shallows
and surrounds brown, crooked reeds scrawled against
    the sky.
I know the rage that builds like these shorter days,
so cold and bitter it burns like nettles at the edges of my
    tongue
and promises nothing but wolf-toothed ice
building a scuffed white ceiling over the pond.
This mean, pitiless day, so cold it sinks to the pond's
    bottom,
freezing the fish in their deep glide and slow, scaly fin-
    sculling,
so it seems as if it will never thaw.

I prefer the rage that builds like storms on humid
    summer nights,
that rises in distant rumbles, cat's paw gusts, and flashes
    lanterning the clouds,
that stretches the air until it throbs and whines like an
    overtightened guitar string,
until gusts lance the swollen heat, and the air is full of
    sound—
rain roaring in the leaves and hissing into the water,
wind whipping green reeds and willow branches to bend
    and lash each other.

It passes with a few last spasms of thunder and rain,
leaving the wrung-out air calm and cool.
First one frog troonks cautiously.
Then the beat begins in earnest,
and peepers sing like spun foil in the dark.

Reading *Moby Dick* on the Farm, 2

Anchored against Ishmael's rage in the lee
of the rough truth of pine bark against my back,
with the honey-and-toast smell of stacked hay
promising harvest closing the year's circle,
buffering me against my own white squalls
and mooring me in the clarity of the farm's strict language
of soil and sowing, harvest and fallow, slaughter and birth,
I see how this countryside seemed to him
a safe harbor with its shallow soundings—
an insular Tahiti, proof against all the terrors of the half-
    known life.
He knew that deep diving and the deeper sea are wedded
    in terror,
that just a spoonful of ocean tastes of God's ferocious
    recklessness.
Nevertheless, he launched himself from the shore,
though the seeming calm and clement sea hid greater
    terrors than storms,
its bland surface shrouding sharkish savagery, demanding
    life's blood,
rendering the level lodestone, map, and sextant useless.
Better to be held in check by marriage, get, and law.
Thus landlocked Nathaniel's story of submission to the A,
of resistance and revolt deferred,
a comfort for him, diving deeper than he knew
himself, drilling further day by day forging a story
that took him and drove him helpless before its gales,
spinning him in its warring currents,
always chasing the leviathan:
God's heartless boast to Job
for which only God can account,
making of a man, wounded and forced to look,
avatar and apotheosis of the truth—

whether mad or bad—that devours sanity,
like Pip, the cabin boy,
our mad captain's only consolation.
Poor Black boy, adrift and alone,
who witnessed the mindless, timeless,
convulsive oceanic nativity
that bred the white beast that became all
that maddens, torments, and cracks the soul
with questions of design or accident
and of the sanity or the madness
of a mind that longs for the one affirming act:
maybe fury's harpoon exploding from an orphaned heart
to strike the beast mortally, to create the man—
ecce homo—
who could dominate him with his rage,
rejecting all the tools of navigation's fantasy
to reveal us in all our naked perplexity;
who with a single stroke could collapse chaos into cosmos;
who would be democrat with the gods
and who suffers his narcissistic crucifixion for all of us,
affirming the freedom of our infinite abandonment,
justifying our pain.

The Green Machine

*"Queequeg no care what god made him shark," . . . agonizingly lifting
his hands up and down; "wedder feejee god or Nantucket god; but de god
wat made shark must be one dam Ingin."*

On the way to the barn to pick up seed
I stop the tractor and kneel to adjust the fan belt.
There's a bright green mantis
beside a field mouse burrow,
her thorn-tipped forelegs raised to the sky.
Under the leaves swaying in the breeze
her compound eyes flicker black
then shoot bright hexagons
as she turns her wedge head left and right.
A mouse edges into the light.
In one sudden lunge she spears it
with barely a bead of blood
and closes her saw-toothed hinges on it,
bends the mouse's head down,
plunges her four mandibles into its neck
and begins to dig in.
The mouse shudders,
seems to collapse into itself,
then lies still in the mantis's vise,
its dulling eyes beyond question.

She finishes, drops the rag of corpse
and climbs to a budding sumac branch.
A spindly male flutters to her
on his four wings' papery rattle
and clasps himself to her back.
He curves his abdomen's tip into hers.
Both begin to pulse like a heartbeat
or an infant's suckling cheeks.

She turns her head around
and eats his head.
The stump of his body
clinches more tightly to her,
still throbbing with life's bumpkin insistence.
And then the male husk
falls away to last year's leaves.
Daintily, she flickers down to it
and finishes her meal to nourish her eggs.

Rufus, the Pig Who Died for Us

Rufus, in spite of being a pig worthy of a name,
a mascot, a friend to all
in a place where most animals had no names
and those that did lived only to labor
was that season's hog.
Rough, wrinkled skin; black, bristly back,
he must have weighed near a half ton.
He stood waist-high,
and he loved to have his back scratched
with the edge of a board,
raising dust.
Eyes squinched
under his flopped ears,
panting with the pleasure of the thing.
He always maneuvered me
between him and the fence
then leaned into me
for more and more
until he was satisfied and trotted away.

Fattening on overripe corn, grain, and slop
through two springs and summers,
friendly and trusting,
he was innocent of his strength.
With one bite
he could slice through
a watermelon rind

Come October
shorter days, longer nights, mists of frost
black ice edging the pond
and in the morning
covering drinking troughs
with the thinnest glass;

42

the best time,
for the cold saves the meat,
thickens the blood.

Rufus was led to a tarp.
He looked around for a treat
or a back-scratch,
eyes squinched
in what I would swear was a smile.
Suddenly shot between the eyes
because fear spoils the meat.

Strung up by his hind legs,
hooked through the tendons,
scalded of his hair,
the remaining tufts scraped away,
he looked naked,
hanging upside-down,
humble as Saint Peter.

We slit his throat
for the blood,
saved for black pudding
or blutwurst.

Then the long cut
hissing from pubis to throat;
then the terrible intimacy
of his innards sliding out
to slop in a wet pile on a tarp.
We separated kidneys,
liver and chitterlings

under his empty body,
dangling, split,
scooped out
to its pearly-pink insides.

So naked.

Porcus dei
qui tollis peccata mundi
ora pro nobis.

Sacrificial
hanging hog of god,
betrayed,
whom we worship
in prospect
for his unctuous belly flesh
cooked crisp and soft
for his rib bones
and their moist, sweet meat,
along ivory's gentle arc,
for his chops, smoked pink,
streaky bacon,
his skin rendered
for crisp chicharrones
and for the diamond-scored fat
of Christmas hams
from his massive thighs
aroma of clove
sharp mustard
brown sugar.

In the old deception
of battening
on spring's glamour
and summer's
fulfillment
and then
in autumn's abundance
lurks winter's treachery
drawn keen
as a bright knife.

Etc.

Maybe I'm rummaging in a dumpster,
mistaking it for an altar,
searching for the true words
that will numb a recollected touch
and drown her sigh
and the white whisper
of her clothes,
her blank eyes
and my yearning terror
in midnights alone that

etch
    my truth's
        razor-
            edge that

sets
    itself
        so deep
            in mind

terror
    rises,
        lava-like,
            then drowns

in dawn's dazzle

becomes an after-
                            thought,

etcetera,

with no one to tell.

Reading *Moby Dick* on the Farm, 3

Odors of balsam and haying
rise in the sinking sun's gold-leaf light and heat
filling this cool green shade,
where I sit,
leaning against this pine's rough factuality,
wild to reach the end of this book,
holding down the unruly pages of his monomania
that drove him day after day to his writing room,
pulling me in his wake to follow him,
deep-diver beneath the placid surface
of this quiet day in the same Berkshires he knew.
Greylock rising green and solid
in the hazy August distance,
seeming as steady and fixed
as somebody's idea of god
and deceptive as the sham of the level line
we draw to navigate between the wound
and belief's soothing balm.
Knowledge seemed a clenched, futile fist shaken
at leviathanic powers
that may bleed only in belief's dream.
In the face of this thunderous **NO**
I'm afraid of losing myself,
plummeting into that endless frenzy
of foaming vortex upon vortex,
deeper than I could sound
with the heaviest lead plummet.

But there are the green, enwombing mountains,
and here is their reflection in this mirroring pond,
and the soothing smell of ripe wheat, cut hay, still water,
mud, frogs and fish, bark and balsam.
How benign the Berkshires must have seemed,
how necessary to cleave to Nathaniel,
to dedicate this hell-fired book to him,
who had learned to use his words
to sail on a steady heading,
no matter how wild the sea and gale,
his poise ballast in that raging storm.
He knew the cost of Nathaniel's serenity.
He saw Nathaniel and himself—
brothers in bearing blackness ten times black,
secretly crying No! in thunder,
knowing all those who say *yes*, lie;
and all those who say *no* live unencumbered
carrying no more baggage
than the strict language
of their reality-creating selves.

Standing Watch

I look, you look, he looks; we look, ye look, they look.

I wait at the top of our west-facing hill
for that single instant that births the dark,
watching sunset's terminator ease up the slope,
proving how the planet rolls.
I shut my eyes.
I open my eyes.
I take a breath.
This rocky, dragon-fanged slope
isn't the same.
And I'm not that one who was standing watch
before that single blink
between inhalation's chill
and exhalation's heat
that carries my voice,
and puffs sloughed cells' clinkers and ash
that ride my breath,
real as my voice is not,
speaking:
"Night,"
and my centripetal gaze
where I stand staring downslope, watching
the swelling dark swallow
the rocks that rip-rap this ridge.

There's a waxing gibbous moon sinking
behind the hump of a hill.
Absolutely still,
not wanting to miss the final sliver's setting,
I stare hard without blinking,
so long that the last of the light
seems to melt and flow along the crest
where a silver swell builds

and breaks against an opal scrim.
I can't tell
whether there's some flaw in my eyes,
or it's the land lolling in its lunar loafing
under the moon's lovely liquefaction
pouring a creamy river over the craggy ridge,
or in this moment
land, moonlight, and I are in cahoots.

I sit on this slope
and dream up her white ghost in the dark,
teetering again on the treacherous cusp of pleasure
I can't contain or name, much less discover
a measure sufficient to parcel it out
while I feel it fill me so full
I'm terrified that to let it bloom
would blast my soul
around the place,
my walls so splintered
I'd be splattered
across this slope, just matter
to be sluiced away with the rain
No matter, simple
as cleaning a slaughterhouse with a steam hose
except for tradition
of words' and cadences' strict order:
ballast and balance in this storm.
Then I might turn away, emptied
and unconsumed by consummation's
munch and guzzle, not yet chewed to mush,
not yet digested, distributed, dispersed,
made no more than nourishment for her ghost,
still the mother and focus of my fury.

Form and Fortress

Words bleed and breathe.
Run your fingers over this page
and taste their pulse,
feel their salty iron stain.
Words might drag me back
to that dazzling white moment,
that woke my rapturous terror
that worms its way into my wall's
fissures and chinks
as winter frost hammers
stones and cracks them wide.

Can I reach back
to rhythm and rhyme
to bind my demi-beast
that wanders this maze,
glamoured by his terror, rage
and desire at that first treachery?

The Minotaur's Sonnet

This sonnet weaves cloth from itself
to clothe its nakedness, searching for its turn
to a lucid ending, only a riff
on redemption that needs to take its turn.
The minotaur rounds another corner,
hoping the way out's hiding in that turn
only to face his naked self and terror,
though entranced by the sight. He wants to turn
away from this brutal charm before he
disappears into himself and returns
to the beast that gnaws him from inside, free

to sing his rough-voiced song that turns
him back to his labyrinth, that will turn
him to that beast. Where is this sonnet's turn?

Couplets

This anger might be mastered on a page.
Rhythm and echo might contain my rage

in this place where wounds throb until the urge
to slaughter memory offers the one purge

possible to wipe away betrayal's
pain and that remembrance that tears and mauls

my memory and my mind and my soul
while I search for the words to make them whole,

that might make midnight's brawling chaos plain
to me, staring, wrapped in what rags remain

of myself. Scattered between love and fear
again, I find myself cringing before

my mover: my feral desire and my rage
that scatters bloody tracks across this page.

Sestina of Rage

I am,
myself, become womb
to a hybrid abomination
which is my fear and rage that feeds
on my blood,
then gets born, thrashing.
It's born, thrashing,
and I am,

myself, the wellspring of the blood
that fills my womb
and feeds
this gluttonous abomination.

This raging abomination
delivers itself, thrashing
and wailing, first feeds
on me until I am,
myself, an empty womb
drained of blood.

Drained of blood
by this mutant abomination,
this wailing child of my womb
that leaves my mind undone and thrashing,
knowing I am,
myself, that burning teat, where he feeds.

My ravenous rage feeds
on my heart's blood.
And I know I am,
myself, this vile abomination
clawing and thrashing
in my terror's womb.

My terror is the womb.
where my rage feeds,
then born howling and thrashing,
slippery with my blood,
this newborn abomination that
I am.

I am, myself, this needy abomination
that feeds on my thrashing rage
and suckles on my own womb's blood.

Nocturne

I'm naked to the bone
With nakedness my shield.
        Theodore Roethke

I come apart as all the armor
of repetition and rhythm fail me,
abandoned and alone in this pitch-dark forest,
naked to the night, naked to the beast:
me, myself, open and exposed.

Night creatures come to the edge
of this clearing where I huddle,
kneeling and curved over myself.
They crouch in the tangle of duff and deadfall
just beyond the glow of the fire that I've kindled
from the remnants of my rage.
They watch me while I stoke the flames
that return in their eyes' green-and-golden flicker.
They back slowly into the dark,
leaving tiny gifts, packets of prey so small
they offer only a taste where my tongue hankers
for blood and meat—
food and the fullness that follows
because a full belly is content and a full mouth
need never speak and only sigh or moan,
unchecked or chopped to words by lips and teeth.

Variations On a Line By Wallace Stevens

Take that, Meister Wallace with your fastidiously fangled feathers

This is old song that will not declare itself
This is old song that will not declare
This is old song that will not
This is old song
This is old
This is
This
Oh!
This
This is
This is old
This is old song
This is old song that declares
This is old song that declares no more
This is old song that declares no more than itself.

55

The Taking

Late August midday and the air's become thick.
The heat sucks color from the fields.
I'm on break, sitting in the barn door's shade,
relaxing into the smell of meal, manure, last year's hay,
spilled motor oil and gasoline.
One-Eyed Howie appears from the darkness in back,
slides down the door, knees splayed, leans back, sighs,
pulls a new pack of Winstons from his shirt pocket,
skins the cellophane,
tears the pack open from the bottom with a yellowed
   thumbnail
so as not to get crud on the filter,
taps a couple out and offers me one.
We smoke, staring out the door
where the land dips past half-filled hayricks
and on into the woods' cool darkness.
Nothing to say about this weather.
Then Howie rolls his good eye to me:

> *"Need your help."*
> *"Okay. . . . What?"*
> *"Got to fix a coupla bulls."*
> *"Why me?"*
> *"Need a big guy."*
> *"Right now?"*
> *"Ayuh."*

At the cattle barn Howie drags a bawling and bucking
   yearling into the corral
by a neck-rope and a finger in each nostril.
He hands me the line.
The little bull pitches back, drags me a few steps.
I dig my boot heels deep into loose, scaly dirt, old shit
   and mud beneath.

From the side, Howie reaches under to the off foreleg,
   suddenly yanks.
The bull falls on his side, rolls on his back.

     "Quick, now.
     Lie on his front end.
     Grab his damn legs."

I feel the bull's chest heaving against my chest.
With each of his forehooves in a hand,
I rise on my toes to bring all my weight down on him.
The bull groans with each breath, snorts, and sprays snot
   in my face.

     "Wait right there.
     Don't let 'im up."

I'm leg-splayed and prone,
my cheek against the bull's wiry hair.
His hot breath smells of grass and grain.
We're like lovers waking at midnight
facing each other, trading breath.
I can't avoid one rolling eye.
I lie on him, one knee hard against his ribs, boot-toes
   dug deep,
the other knee breaking through the dirt-crust,
mud, piss, and shit soaking through my jeans.
His forelegs heave, almost lift me.
His split hoof digs into my ribs, peels skin
where sweat rolling down my side stings.

Howie appears with a bottle of pine tar disinfectant.
He squats at the ass-end,
framed in the hind legs' vee.
He smiles and reaches into his shirt pocket,

takes out a single-edge Gem razorblade.
He cups the bull's gray-haired scrotum in his palm,
delicately pinches the base so one testicle bulges,
takes the blade, slices the tender purse,
squeezes, and a pearly, blue-marbled oval pops out,
dangles from a stringy, white cord.
Piss fountains and splashes across my back.

     "Hold him, now!
     Hold him down, dammit!"

The bull bellows, breaking falsetto.
I can't look away. No shifting,
sprawled on his forelegs,
so close I can see a swollen tick on his chest.

The heat falls like a hammer.
I'm gasping with the bull.
The corners of my tongue fizz with copper
and my temples feel stuffed with cotton.
Black spots flutter like moths,
spiral in from the corners of my sight.
My gut feels empty,
at the same time packed with slimy ice.
Howie daintily shaves the cord. It parts.
He weighs the ivory, blue-veined jelly in his palm,
puts it aside on a wood plank.

     "Save it for later.
     Bread it.
     Fry it up."

He does the same thing on the other side,
turns and reaches for the pine tar.

Between the hind legs two red holes pulse
like gouged, astonished eyesockets.
Howie pours black, thick pine tar into each wound.
Suddenly, I'm breathing the sweet smell of balsam
and the metallic smell of blood.
The steer bucks. I'm tossed away.

I rise to my feet, slip to one knee
catch myself on my hands,
and stumble to the gate,
slip the leather thong holding it shut and pass through
on legs that may as well be stone for all they bend
or how much my feet feel the ground,
wavering toward the woods' cool, dark green.

> "Hey! Hey!
> Where you goin'?
> Hey!
> Get back here.
> 'Nother to do."

I don't turn.
I raise one hand and keep on.
Howie laughs and laughs.
And I walk into piney shade
until his laughter tangles in the wild grapevines and
    deadfall.
Somehow I'm sitting, leaning against a tree,
my fingers buried in dirt and last year's brown leaves,
me, stinking of sweat, piss, sunbaked shit, blood, and
    pine tar,
driving my fingers into the soft forest duff,
trying to grow roots.

Ambergris

*Now that the incorruption of this most fragrant ambergris should be
found in the heart of such decay; is this nothing?*

Astonishing, that a speck of sand,
rough beyond remedy
will work its slow way

into pale, tender flesh,
until agony declares itself
in lunar radiance.

The soft meat flinches.
As the grain drives deep,
slow nacre surrounds it.

When the shell is pried open,
the meat cringes in the sun's glare,
revealing its secret glory in blush and opal.

Astonishing, ambergris
is something swallowed,
so loathy and vomitous

the deep-diving whale
carries the cramp
curdling in its gut

until it's puked
or shat out.
The whale swims on,

leaving behind floating,
foul, excremental,
gray-black-streaked pudding.

Then air, sun, and saltwater's seethe
makes a gift of it—
waxy perfume, balm, and ease.

So strange that spewed agony
might become attar and balm
to soothe and smother the flame

while my rage tears at my gut.
It will not be magicked
to soft glow or floating treasure.

Reading *Moby Dick* on the Farm, 4

I'm sitting by the pond
where the woods edge the shore,
my back against a pine, cool in its shade,
reading the last few pages of this hell-fired book.
And here, now, afloat in harvest smells,
I'm cradled in the Berkshires, near Arrowhead,
where, like Odysseus, he carried his oar,
to write far from the sea,
under Greylock's dark and rocky brow.
He settled only a few miles from Nathaniel:
whose heart he wished would beat next to his.
Nathaniel's puzzled, careful regard,
perplexed at his need, god-estranged
to embrace them, together, as one,
and so mend the fragments of the godhead
in his searching for words,
solid and exact, that might speak true
for belief, or unbelief.

Letter to Barbara, Never Sent

Yesterday, I got a letter from an old friend
whose agony at remembering her father's touch
had driven her into solitary, mute madness.

Maybe something else is going on.
I haven't spoken out loud in over four years.
Some email threads feel like speech.
Wish I could talk to you.
Last saw my kids in 2013.
Go figure.
I moved to Uruguay.
Better than suffering here.
Life is better but still lonely.
You can't talk to me?

Maybe something else is going on.
I've had my doubts, too,
suspecting the specious surface of things.
You've always been too smart
to take the mirror
of the deep blue dome webbed with cirrus
and its watery twin streaked
with white windrift on its face
for reality.
You're too true not to look closely,
like listening through a tune
for its real, diabolic ostinato.

I haven't spoken out loud in over four years.
Holy sister of agony,
you've taken a vow of silence,
knowing words are sound and breath
chopped and shaped by teeth and tongue
to embody the veiling light,

being only words, only wind,
temporary and transient.
They may not surrender or surround.
They may obscure the vision
that longs to dive deep,
to see through sea's sapphire face
or its sister in the firmament's dome
to wrench out the creator's face,
or if there's nothing there,
to rest in that truth.

Some email threads feel like speech.
We speak,
string words into nets
meant to trap
our deep-sea life
that writhes away.
Another answers and another
until we're strangled and breathless,
meshed and helpless to speak or swim,
and so we sink.

Last saw my kids in 2013.
I know the madness that warps
love to rage, terrifying
in what it may drive us to.
And love cuts the lines
when we need to leave the lee
of home and the fireside
or risk our rage destroying them,
and so we slip the anchor
and give ourselves
to our currents and winds
mad or bad as they may be.

Go figure.
Figure:
   reckon,
      guess,
         believe,
            think,
               suppose,
                  presume,
                     assume
It all slips away.
Rock-hard certainty, helpless
against the amoebic shape of dreams,
protozoan, first life, original,
the formless jelly laid down
in primal ooze that cannot be netted,
slips through words' interstices.
Go figure,
a useless attempt
to catch the beast.

I moved to Uruguay.
Better than suffering here.
Life is better but still lonely.
Odysseus, returned from ten years' wandering,
surviving cyclops, the wandering stones,
and especially sinister Circe
who turned beautiful,
bountiful lust to swinish filth.
He slaughtered Penelope's suitors,
reclaimed his home, his line, his family,
only to give it up and wander again
so far inland he was anonymous
and the sea was no more than a myth.

You can't talk to me?
No, I can't talk to you.
We share too much to talk,
and if we did,
our wounds would bleed
into each other.
When it's too clear to look,
we turn inward and away,
curl into a hollow in the woods
and suckle on our pain and rage
until they fill us to the brim,
and to speak to another or
even give sound to our voice
might be the deadly salve and balm
to heal the wound and quiet the rage
that gives us breath and form.
Comforted, we'd be empty,
so we choose the demoniac frenzy,
self-cast adrift, longing and fearful
of the damage we imagine
that we might do,
might want to do,
affirmed, alone, in an alien land,
alien to everything but ourselves.

The Unhealing Wound

. . . then it was, that his torn body and gashed soul bled into one another;
and so interfusing, made him mad. . . . So man's insanity is heaven's
sense; and wandering from all mortal reason, man comes at last to that
celestial thought, which, to reason, is absurd and frantic. . . .

He lived in the world, as the last of the Grisly Bears lived in settled
Missouri. And as when Spring and Summer had departed, that wild
Logan of the woods, burying himself in the hollow of a tree, lived out the
winter there, sucking his own paws; so, in his inclement, howling old age,
Ahab's soul, shut up in the caved trunk of his body, there fed upon the
sullen paws of its gloom!

1.

My father had diabetes
out of the self-devouring
rage of the Jew
to slaughter the enemy
who had broken the world he'd loved
until it drove him away,

returned to Germany
to see in the skeletal faces
the spidery begging hands,
the eyes blank with hopelessness
what might have been his end.

Out of his bleak rages
he searched out his death,
embracing all that pain
with a sugary fuck you
of denial's diabetic defiance.
At least he could rush into rot.
This, at least, was his own.

And he owned the wounded leg
that would not heal,
its gaping red mouth
muzzled under stained bandages,
skin darkening to the shade of dead fires;
then, the sweet, retching reek of rotting pork.

What do they do with an amputated limb?
Tossed in a morgue freezer
with the rest of that day's reaping,
incinerated every evening
in a white-tiled hospital basement.

It rises in smoke and ashes from a tall brick stack,
drifting over summer Central Park,
promiscuous with the other leavings, unnoticed.
Smoke and ashes, floating
over the peace that comes with the cooling day,
over lengthening tree shadows
stretched over privet and grass, maple and gingko,

settling on reluctant children heading home,
on businessmen, their jackets slung over their shoulders
and their ties unknotted and dangling,
on old people nodding out on benches,
on arm-and-leg-twined lovers on blankets,
all ignorant of the furnace and the flames—
the faintest white dusting,
too soft to feel, too fine to see.

2.

Ahab has a wound that will not heal
himself, abused, abandoned child,
turned vulture in his anguished rage,
tearing at his stumped and thwarted love,
affirmed by the lacerating revelation
that smashed the creed of commerce—
trade, balance, profit, loss, mensuration, and calibration—
to reveal the rough wrong of the beast.
Left with a phantom limb's agony
that scorches his nights and lights his dreams,
slung in his hammock,
his brain burnt to bare rock,
he's numb to the motherly lullaby of the ship
swaying on the rock and stroke of the sea.

In his sleep he mumbles the words of mastery;
his hands grasp at the tools of his trade:
spermaceti, whalebone, ambergris,
harpoon, lance, flensing knife, trypots
mainsail, top sail, topgallant sail,
lee side, weather side
whaleboat, oar and line.
And all the holy terms of the hunt
become simply breathy sound,
words, whispers, flimsy scrims,
wind-ravaged and torn away like his leg
to reveal his helpless lust and bottomless rage.

How is it that agony may become a self
and pain become its own justification?
He's become his own demoniac image of despair
for if a beast can scythe away a limb, simply bestial,
then there's no sense behind the firmament
or the mirrored surface of the sea's blue,
only an opaque copy of the sky,
the myth of the divine metallurge's dome of the firmament,
created to separate pure heaven from corrupt earth,
suddenly metallic blue, only a reflection
concealing a void, empty of sense.
And belief burnt to smoke and ashes
rises with the sooty, stinking smoke
of the try-pots rendering blubber
blows away in the wind.

.

Winter Morning

I woke up early
in the frozen morning twilight
and made my way
through my parents' home.
I caught a glimpse
through their barely open bedroom door.
Dad sat on the edge of their bed,
my mother only a blanketed hump.
He never saw me peering in,
too sunk in his loss,
getting ready to dress and go to work.
He wore a singlet and boxers
and the tapered stump below his right knee
dangled while he caressed the thigh,
so wasted, barely thicker than his femur.
And all the time,
hunched over that fraction
he shook his head over and over
in the soiled winter light.

The Pulpit

It'll be a little soggy but just keep slogging.
We'll soon be on dry ground."
We were, waist deep in the Big Muddy
And the big fool said to push on.
      Pete Seeger

Father Mapple, ancient child,
his faith shines over his congregation
of sailors sheltered from the storm
that blurs the stained-glass light
and pummels the church.
Cold drafts swirl through strained seams
and shingles lift and spin away through the squall.
He climbs to his pulpit
in the shape of ship's bluff bow,
alone, high above the congregation,
where he looks down upon them.
He mounts by a rope ladder.
He pulls it up behind him.
The figurehead is a crucifix.
The lectern is the bowsprit
that thrusts forward,
bearing the weight of the Word
cantilevered in empty air.
It shadows the sailors seated below
hands folded in their laps
or palm to palm in prayer,
eyes raised toward his words that seem
to them to fall in sapphire light
breaking through heaped clouds.
Belief's avatar
sworn to comfort sailors' doubt,
he sermons them to faith
gazing down from his bow-world-pulpit.

He will not sail by dead reckoning
but by the lodestone needle of the Book
and the sextant of doctrine,
prizing out the navigating stars
from the chaos of the night-tempest.
Travel speaks of Jonah's agony,
beaten and buffeted in his soul's storm,
Jonah, become a name for cursed luck,
cast into the sea and swept away ahead of an oily calm
swallowed and then birthed from leviathan's belly,
vomited up like ambergris
sweetened by faith's false fragrance.
And he leaves his pulpit and his assembly.
Lost.

Blues for Pip: Introduction

Pip was the Black cabin boy—servant to all aboard the *Pequod*, doomed ship in *Moby Dick*.

> *Poor Alabama boy! On the grim Pequod's forecastle, ye shall ere long see him, beating his tambourine; prelusive of the eternal time, when sent for, to the great quarter-deck on high, he was bid strike in with angels, and beat his tambourine in glory; called a coward here, hailed a hero there!*

Pip was pressed into service into the crew of Stubb, the second mate's, whaleboat when one of the oarsmen was injured. In the great chase, the harpooner, Tashtego, struck a whale, and boat and crew were taken on a Nantucket sleigh ride. Pip panicked and jumped overboard. Stubb cut the line to rescue Pip. Stubb told Pip the next time he wouldn't stop for him and lose a whale. Soon after, the same event occurred, and true to his word, Stubb left Pip floating in the open ocean, assuming the following whaleboats would pick him up. They did not.

Floating alone in the horizonless ocean, Pip, unequal to the truth, was granted Ishmael's and Ahab's vision:

> *Pip's ringed horizon began to expand around him miserably. By the merest chance the ship itself at last rescued him; but from that hour the little negro went about the deck an idiot; such, at least, they said he was. The sea had jeeringly kept his finite body up, but drowned the infinite of his soul. Not drowned entirely, though. Rather carried down alive to wondrous depths, where strange shapes of the unwarped primal world glided to and fro before his passive eyes; and the miser-merman, Wisdom, revealed his hoarded heaps; and among the joyous, heartless, ever-juvenile eternities, Pip saw the multitudinous, God-omnipresent, coral insects, that out of the firmament of waters heaved the colossal orbs. He saw God's foot upon the treadle of the loom, and spoke it; and therefore his shipmates called him mad. So man's insanity is heaven's sense; and wandering from all mortal reason, man comes at last to that celestial thought, which, to reason, is absurd and frantic; and weal or woe, feels then uncompromised, indifferent as his God.*

Blues for Pip

> *. . . and they saw the God of Israel; and there was under His feet the like*
> *of a paved work of sapphire stone, and the like of the very heaven for*
> *clearness.*

Am I blue, am I blue
Ain't these tears in my eyes telling you
Am I blue, you'd be too . . .

Last night in my sleep I heard your tambourine,
Heard its jingle-jangle and sank down in that dream.
Dreamed of you in darkness and heard your tambourine.
Saw you dance ahead of me in the midnight-starlight sheen.

Saw you dancing down a road to that never-ending black.
Yes, you led me down the road to that soul-devouring black.
The dust beneath my feet showed your footprints' fading track.
And I knew that if I followed you, I wasn't coming back.

Then I wrapped my arms around you and, loving, took you in.
I bound and soothed your wounds and gently let you in.
'Cause we're tossed into the void, and horror wears our skin.
And I knew I shared your terror, and, loving, took you in.

You whispered me your secrets and offered me your eyes,
Your eyes that saw the emptiness that hides behind the lies.
You tore me through the paper walls printed with those lies
and shared your godless vision that purifies our eyes.
>   *Anonymous*

Is blue the word for holiness,
or the lacquer we lay on the void?
The colored and coloring glasses
that keep us from gazing ourselves blind
at the white shroud that wraps all?

We paint Rama and Krishna blue.
The blue Buddha is the healer.

The Virgin Mary wears blue,
the color of the queen of heaven,
the color of god's sapphire pavement,
the color of humanity free of flesh's flaw,
the color of Advent's natal hope,
renewal, rebirth, the good news,
the color of the morning star,
the color of clement sea and sky.

Is blue the color of divinity
or just the rarest color in nature,
the most expensive pigment
we slather on a blank canvas
to prettify the divine deception?

Everywhere above
the sun-filled sky scatters
white light's blinding colorless all-color
and returns bamboozling blue.

Poor Pip.
He was a cabin boy,
happy as his tambourine's jangle
lighting his little, sunless realm.
Black boy with the lowest share—
from steerage to forecastle
he knew his place.

Then he had a glimpse
beneath the endless blue plain
reflecting the dome of blue;
and the visions that rose before him,
beyond the limits of his mind,
forced huge, unwanted knowledge

that cramped and swelled in him,
came to term, and birthed dread.
So, he sees and speaks his terror's wisdom.
Pip, terrorized, only is escaped to tell us
how he has himself become a terror.

Here is his story:
Pip, born to serve belowdecks,
artless and alien tenant of the margins,
bullied to the sunny deck, taken
to fill an empty seat in the perilous pageant-hunt.
Terror froze him
webbed in the whale-line
under leviathan's mauling, scything tail
hovering above the matchstick boat.
And the memory of words
boomed out in landlocked churches
echoed his dread.

> *Canst thou draw out leviathan with an hook? or*
> *his tongue with a cord which thou lettest down?*
> *Canst thou put an hook into his nose? or bore his*
> *jaw through with a thorn?*
> *Canst thou fill his skin with barbed irons? or his*
> *head with fish spears?*
> *None is so fierce that dare stir him up: who then is*
> *able to stand before me?*

Abandoning his oar to escape
the harpoon line's frenzied hiss
he jumped into the boundless blue.

Adrift, he floated mouth-deep,
water-gagged, salt-stung where the oar had blistered him.
Ignorant of the sea beyond god's arrogant brag,

he came to know his abandonment
as the whaleboats disappeared over Earth's curve.
Orphaned, he searched the sky for a face,
found only a sapphire blank,
listened for that churched voice,
heard only the blue surrounding sea
whispering his insignificance in his ears.
Alone and silent under the expanding horizon,
frantically paddling to raise his head,
he tired, submitted, then floated, arms spread
jacket billowing on the water like flukes,
free and alone,
without a human voice.
And then he sank.

And then he saw

> the god-omnipresent coral insects that heaved the
> colossal spheres from the firmament of waters.

or god's omnifictive moral precepts
that hide barbarity's atrocious, reciprocating truths in
    words
that lurk under faith's fatal sapphire skin.

And then he knew
that neither water nor land
that god is said to have divided on the second day
nor the rough creatures of the sea scuffing his bare,
    frantic feet
that god is said to have created on the third day
regarded him as important,
nor did the huge voice ringing its idiot yammer in his ears
over and over:

Who, then, is able to stand before me?

He discovered rage
who had never known
the right to rage,
wished for a weapon
to destroy the temples
and then it came to him:
No weapons. No temples.
No ordnance, no target
adequate to his rage.

Rescued, finally,
by the white-winged ship
following its children,
Pip, poor mind-flayed cabin boy,
made unwilling prophet,
stripped of belief's sheltering pelt,
all raw nerve and agony at a touch
on his soul's pulsing wound,
like a gash revealing raw flesh
spoke his vision to his shipmates.
And for this they called him mad, or bad,
for revealing celestial stagecraft,
birthing knowledge that sours, sears
and withers mortal reason to wretched terror.

Is the color of god blue
or just a hue,
indifferent and dividing
the idea of heaven from earth's fact—
color of desperation and a void?

Blue is a word, empty air
shaped by cheeks, lips, and tongue,
a word for a color, arbitrary, no more
than all light sponged up
but for a wavelength flung back,
a challenge to make meaning
from cosmic cosmetic's cheat:
knowing's fundamental instant.
Blue:
Only a word.
It may not surrender
or surround
the truth,

Pip, me, I, we, us, infidel, sinner,
unwilling prophet gazing into shadows,
gazing himself blind and deaf
at that blank wall.
tainted by knowledge
like white eyes that gaze into him.
He is the speaking scar
that no one dares confront.
They turn from him and the vision,
forced beneath the sapphire delusion
of the arcing firmament's glory
and its reflection in the sea—
essential blood,
womb-stuff, water,
deceitful mother.
Water is all
there is
where there is
water

struck mindless from the blast's first flare
when the shocked void swelled
with the amniotic surge
where the cabin boy abandoned
in the universe of waters
and uncertainty's flux
the vertiginous exile
remembers his home
and discovers abandonment
far from where god
like a smith fashioned
the waters into a cobalt dome
out of the forge of his will
and named it firmament
to divide brief flesh
from eternal soul
the boy is overcome
by water pouring
from the first eruption,
separated from the crimson
universe of blood.
All is water
is all
there is
there is
no water
nowhere—
universe's
universal solvent
suspended
and in flux,
everywhere.

He learns hate and rage at the injustice
of knowledge that uncovers the delusion
that wounds and scars with the agony
of wearing two faces—
the face of what he'd lost
and the truer face of what he'd become
bearing the scar of truer knowledge
tangled in that white beast.

All of this, being words,
may not be true,
may not surrender
or surround
the truth,
yet it is all the truth
Pip can speak
of doctrine's stink
and the outhouse reek
of doctrine's cheat
and our long despair.

Pip, me, I, we, us, infidel, sinner, prophet
gazing into shadows.

Ahab Dreams of Home. . .

Oh, Starbuck! it is a mild, mild wind, and a mild looking sky. . . . Why this strife of the chase? why weary and palsy the arm at the oar, and the iron, and the lance?

My wife, my love, my victim,
I'd lived alone too long in a rented room,
where the night wind whispering through the window,
over my narrow, single-dented bed;
hove to against the storm of my insomniac solitude,
finally soothed to sleep by buoy bells
that rocked in the sway of the swells at the swerve of the tide.

Then you rescued me, my lee harbor, my sheltering cove,
gifted me with the blessings of your innocence:
safety, comfort, homely food, warm blankets, friends;
the heart, the bed, the table, the fireside, the hearthstone
in a land where I could sink a fencepost
and raise our child, our mortal guarantee.

Then the unhealing wound driving me,
navigating past all the charts
into the horizonless, mapless white blank
to create god and justice out of my rage,
leaving me lost, drifting here, who-knows-where,
dismasted, with phantom fangs gnawing my lost leg's length.
My only comfort's the polar reason
forced on an illiterate Black cabin boy
tortured by visions beyond his simple reach.
I've taken him in as poultice to my wound.
He speaks celestial thought, futile and frantic,
a solace to me, self-proclaimed lord of the level lodestone
who destroyed my sextant and my compass.

Sea fog rises tonight, eating the horizon and the stars.
And I,   I,   I,   I
sail by dead reckoning,
which I fear now is too true,
staring at the place where the horizon's denied me,
staring till my eyeballs ache,
becalmed by rage in a Sargasso of need.

I drown in fear, fury, and the desire
to front that faceless, bluff, blank white wall
and flukes that churn the water to bright, white curds,
pushing a blazing, foam-edged wave before,
glittering and flushed in the setting sun, red as my rage.
Then I, mindless lover,
driven to the catastrophic recognition
of mine own, my lust and rage
pouring from my bucking hips, harpooned
into that void, filled with time's babble.

But now September haying's golden odor
blows across the water
from some far inland, upland field,
full of crickets' creak
and wheat's rustle in a breeze.
All, all of it speaks to me of home, of our broad bed,
how it warmed and swaddled us like a downy breast.
All, all of the sweet, warm benediction
of your arms clasped around my neck,
of your heels knotted against my back,
speaks of how you taught me love's sanctified dance,
speaks of how you clenched me
to the loamy land and the sweet fulfillment
of my years' autumnal swing.

You rise before me this night
with the odor of lavender and verbena
and the secure and sacred warmth of grain laid by
in dim winter barns,
bounded by a horizon that doesn't pitch and waver.

If I return,
I'll take you and our child and an oar
and limp inland, far beyond the sound of the sea,
mine own Odysseus,
to a place where they don't know
the why of oars or ships
or of whalebone legs
but only of harvest and winnowing
in golden fall's merciful light.

No more whiplashed back to sea again,
to perform my death-drama with the great grave beast
that drives me from your safe harbor
chasing the monster—
riddle and answer
to ruined, wounded,
god-flimflammed Job.

Oh, but I'm girdled by this narrow oaken stage
where I act out this ancient script in foreknown words,
self-gaffed, hauled by my tongue and lip,
to speak the universal rage that bends men to my will.
Their surrender stokes the fire of this absent leg
and feeds that furnace that leaves me
soot-stained, burnt to an atom in the same flames
that redden the clouds' sagging bellies, heavy with storm
to render leviathan's monstrous bulk to soothing unguent
that will ease my rage, that will tell me who I am

and calm the frenzied chop of my mind,
like god's blessed oil anointing Jonah's storm
and grant me the completion of this haying's harvest
and the laying by in the expectation of spring.

Hay Rake

*They have been making hay somewhere under
the slopes of the Andes, Starbuck, and the mowers
are sleeping among the new-mown hay.*

I squint into the late September setting sun,
clinging to a bouncing, bare-metal saddle
welded to an S-shaped, flat, iron bar
welded to a hay-rake aged to black,
hitched by a four-by-four tongue to a rust and primer-gray
   truck.
The rake's steel-spoked wheels wobble on their axle,
pounding and crashing over buried rocks and old furrows.
Behind me eighteen curved tines thrash cut hay into a
   hissing spindle.
Evening draws down and eases from the woods,
pours into hollows, and rises around hummocks.
Dust, hay-shards, and seed float behind me in a pink
   contrail,
slip up my nose, past my collar, and stick to my sweaty back.
With both hands white-knuckled to the saddle,
I can't reach behind to scratch, and I don't dare sneeze,
not with the chance of falling back on the teeth
or spilling forward to run spraddle-legged over the tongue,
one hand cupping my balls, the other desperately waving,
praying the driver sees me or the empty seat
before we U-turn at the field's edge.

Now, the hay's filled the rake just right,
building and spinning like a breaking wave.
I stamp on the stirrup-shaped pedal by my right heel.
The teeth whip up, clang against the seat, whip down.
If I do this at just the right time,
I scribe a straight line across the field,
rose-gold and edged with black in the sunset slant.

We pelt into our long shadow and wheel around at the
    field's end.
I lean into the turn, loving the skill of balancing
my weight against the turn's outward pull.
My metal fingers fall, grab the next hanks of hay.

We're cruising now into the low, tree-laced sun on our
    last run.
I relax into the bump and flex, knowing that we're about
    done
and then I'll stand in this final field
while the dwindling day shadows the stubble
that speaks of the plenty in the hayloft.

The field will darken as the evening breeze rises
and the trees will take a huge breath,
to return it in a slow, soothing sigh
as I slip into an autumn dream
of how this night Orion and his dogs
will rise and hunt across the frost-fogged sky,
how the little dipper will pivot around Polaris,
telling all the time in the world,
and how I'll turn in my bed and inhale the scent
of sweet hay drying and autumn's promise of completion.
I believe I'll dream of moony clouds rolling in the wind's
    rake,
leaving perfectly straight silver strokes across night's
    black field.

Reading *Moby Dick* on the Farm, 5

I sit here in this cool green shade,
bathed in odors of balsam and haying,
gilded in sinking gold-leaf light,
leaning against a pine trunk's rough truth,
ignoring promises made and chores postponed
to reach the end of this book,
holding down the rebellious pages
of that uncontainable obsession
that drove him day after day to his writing room,
driving me to follow him,
deep-diver beneath the placid surface
of this quiet day among the unchanging Berkshires
rising green in the hazy August afternoon distance,
seeming steady and immovable
as somebody's idea of god
and deceptive as the soothing line
drawn between doctrines and justice.
Then, truth's despairing rage
is a futile fist, clenched bloodless, shaken
at the pale incarnation of leviathanic power
that may suffer and bleed only in belief's dream;
at the same time, fearful
that to get lost in meditation
ends with plummeting
into that endless maelstrom
of vortex upon vortex,
deeper than I could sound
with the heaviest lead plummet.

Nocturne: Ishmael Alone

Wachet auf ruft uns die stimme.
De profundis clamavi ad te, Domine

It's night in the forecastle.
The sailors sleep in their bunks
like the dead awaiting resurrection,
heads bowed to knees curled to chest,
backs against the ship's curved oak skin
where it tapers to the blunt prow
that shoves the icy, corpse-cold waves away
and shoulders pale-eyed ghosts aside,
though they reach with bony hands
to stall the ship and pull it down.
Here they sleep,
their dreams stoked and haunted
by cetacean moans and trills.
I remain wakefully watchful over these innocents
under the flicker of a dimming lantern
gimballed from the ceiling.
Swinging in the surge of the squall and the sea,
it paints the walls with shadows
against the bowed bow in endless revision.
Shapes seem to form and reform
amorphous as breath, ephemeral as words.
And here I sit, unsleeping, squatting over a foot locker
under the smoky, swaying light,
my eyes gritty and my throat raw with smoke.
I, Ishmael (Me, He, Him, Pip, Us) write,
trying to web the leviathan
in a net of arbitrary words.
I wonder: how do scrawls contain sounds?
And how do the same line of scrawls

become different—arbitrary as
Thought:
      Tough
            Through
                  Plough
                        Though
                              Cough
and how can the same idea spoken
differently by different
men in different languages,
all of them partakers of the hunt
make meaning?

Whale
   Wal
      Hval
         Hvalur
            Valas
               Keath
                  Kujira
                     Jing Yu
                        Balena

How do I net thought with such uncertain tools?
What seine is sufficient unto the task?
Words being no more than breath
shaped by lips and tongue
haphazard sounds, arbitrary,
gauzy as smoke rising from this lantern
drifting out through the hatch.
Hunkered in the hull's depths,
I (Me, He, Him, Pip, Us) write, trying to surround
the leviathan that swims in night's abyss
dreaming and dreamt, eternally there.

Incidental Divinity

It's late in the season for mowing,
but we've neglected an outlying field
carved from the woods,
planted with rye to be mowed
and plowed under for spring.
I've been sent out alone this morning
on our beat-up, red-and-rust Farmall Cub,
proud to be trusted.

At the end of the field
I lower the mower blades
and engage the power take-off.
The hiss and clatter of cutting rye
rises around me
along with dust and stalk fragments.
My track is like the wake
of a ship tacking into a stiff wind.

The mower stutters,
and the engine
coughs,
coughs,
picks up again.
There's a splatter of blood on my hand.
Cold in my gut, I slam the ignition off,
stumble from the still-coasting tractor.

Here's a big woodchuck.
Half its head is gone.
It paws at the air.
A ruby pool puddles under it.
I look around for a sharp tool,
a spade, anything to chop with;
I think of stomping it.

But it stops in mid-stride,
seems to shrink.

The surrounding woods swell and gray.
I can't breathe.
Then I remember how.
I knuckle my eyes,
climb back in the saddle
and finish the job.

For days after
I can find the body by its rank stink.
I return to the field, staring
at the rice-grain maggots
pouring from its mouth like true speech
and writhing in its ragged eyeholes.

With each visit, the chuck seems to collapse,
folding into other dimensions;
hunks of matted fur,
rags of blackened skin,
yellow teeth, ivory bones.

By January there are only
a few disarticulated bones
and brittle, ice-crusted pelt,
hard as iron when I poke it with my toe,
winter-welded to the stony soil.

One March night I drop to my hands and knees,
nose close to the softening ground:
an animal, maybe a coyote,
sniffing at the strewn ruins.
Only the lush smell of thawing mud.

Sent to harrow the field in April
I fire up the Cub.
In one spot there is a greener hummock,
ecstatic with the flicker
of crimson clover,
cornflower, and buttercup.
The morning light picks out
a boiling swarm of gnats,
and a hunting swallow's eccentric circle.

The Outhouse

The scriptures dwell in duality.
Be beyond all opposites, Arjuna:
anchored in the real, and free
from all thoughts of wealth and comfort.
  The Bhagavad Gita. *trans. Stephen Mitchell*

An outhouse forgives all sins without confession.
  Robert Wrigley

Here I am at the edge of the furthest field,
sitting hunkered in the dark,
alone in this fundamental moment,
faced with a dark, wooden wall shoved close,
a screen for my doubts' parade
while I squat above this ancestral-human stench,
lost in the earth's miasmic truth that rises from the pit.
How is this not penance enough to earn shriveness,
or at least something like knowledge?

And there's the stack of newsprint,
so when my rage gets the better of me,
my only comfort is wiping my ass with the words
of presidents and statesmen, divines and barefaced prophets,
crumpling shit-smeared opinions, history and theology
to be dropped into a hole, reeking of annals and chronicles,
theories, explanations, revelations, arguments, white papers
placations, compromises, surrenders, refusals, manifestos:
all those delusions and the glittering assurances of doctrine.
Here, the putrid truth rises and reveals itself
in this twilight where learning
and relearning my place in this place
is sufficient contrition.

Then, penitent and purged of purpose and plan,
I find that squatting in this warm half-dark

surrounded by the summer sound of bees
working over blooming flowers
drawing honey from this fetid, fecund soil,
or under spring rain's spatter spilling over warped shingles
and down gapped siding,
raising the smell of old oak and new growth,
or listening to birds' spring doxologies in greeny shade,
or feeling the first cold breath of autumn's flow and flux
between opening winter and the last of summer,
full of the smell of burning leaves
easing under the hinge-sprung door
and through the crescent cut-out
is salvation enough.

The Outhouse: Epilogue

So, Pip finally knew,
and spoke
for us, too.
When he saw through
the swindle of blue,
he granted us
the speechless vision
of season and sprout
and taught us to submit
to the will of the worm
that wipes words' flimsy walls away
along with all impediment,
channeling sense
to nerve
to mind
until the world is one
fluorescing,
deliquescing,
coalescing joy,
encompassing
droplet and ocean,
eon and nanosecond,
speaker and spirit,
origin and ending
mutually contained,
in me and you
as when I see the whole
gritty, glowing world
in these places.

Reading *Moby Dick* On the Farm, 6

Finding myself for some seasons on a farm
to exhume and exorcise the pale bitch
and learn the healing language of planting and reaping,
how the line of any life bends to the healing seasons' circle,
containing slaughter's and blood's necessary conditions
the canons and fugues of sowing and harvest
playing against seasons' rondo of turn and return;
fallow and compost; harrow and sow, bud and sprout:
the immensity of a thready, bone-pale stem
unfurling its first green leaf
the sharp press of autumn's stubble through my boot soles;
the momentous struggle of a newborn lamb nuzzled by its
    mother,
kicking free of its caul to stand for the first time
wobbling on reedy legs nosing against her udder;
the milky smell of winter calves safe in their stalls
and hay's summer scent drifting from the hayloft
against frost's struck flint-smell outside,
learning the inconsequence of any single life
and the consequence of pigs' daily slop
collected from the evening kitchen.

Slopping the Pigs,
Ending With a Line by Emerson

White cheese rinds, bright as diamonds,
emerald and ruby watermelon rinds,
topaz carrot tops, brown-edged lettuce leaves,
all suspended in a thick, pale, stinking soup
of discarded cereal and souring milk,
floating brown clots of cold gravy,
fat trimmings, pale rags of raw chicken skin,
soaked loaf ends and bread-crust mush,
sloshing over the rims of dented garbage cans.
I'm splattered with swill and coated with road dust
bouncing down this dirt road in the back of a stakebed truck
hauling dinner to the pigs.

I heft a can and tip it into the splintered wooden trough.
Clouds of flies rise in this evening's cooling air
as if that glutinous stink were alive.
Tangled in the scuffle, snort, and squeal of hungry pigs
that unravels into satisfied, comfortable grunting;
standing among stubborn burdock and purslane
growing from the muddy muck of mud,
spilled slops, last night's rain, and pig shit,
all of it copper-barred and glowing like hot coals
in the cooling air and sunset's pine-sliced slant,
it comes to me:
I am part and parcel of god.

Fluorescence, Deliquescence Coalescence, Fluorescence

Fluoresce, deliquesce, coalesce, fluoresce—living in
the middle of the divine friction of things inhabiting
each other, streaming light down nerves' threads and
unbinding the soul's strictures.

Yesterday I saw a dying bee, ground-bound, struggling,
its abdomen writhing, staggering toward a yellow
dusting of pollen by a fallen sprig of wilting privet
flowers.

She fell, lay still for a time, roused and staggered a few
inches more, collapsed on scattered petals and gold
grains by the brittle twig, became still.

And she comes to mind this morning while I walk my
neighborhood before sunrise, easing myself through
the last of the dark.

Overhead, a salmon-pink contrail, sunrise-stained,
seems to draw itself

from nothing to nothing, and then the gnat at its head
flashes in the oblique sun, still below my horizon.

Now the sun first strikes the top of our ridge, then crawls
down the blue-green serpentine and grass, pouring
over houses, trees and yards, then warm on my face.

The plane enters a different climate, loses its trail,
becomes a dull speck fading into the blue as its far
mumble, drawn thin as molten glass, tapers to silence.

A murder of crows flutters down to roadkill on the
street.

One perches high on a telephone pole crosspiece keeping
watch while I pass under,

cocks a black sequin eye down at me, caws once, decides
to ignore me and hunkers down, waiting his turn.

Among a liquidambar's five-point leaves doused in
  golden light, a red-tail hawk clutches a sprawled dove
  to a branch with her scaly talons.
She dips her beak to its chest, plucked naked-pink and
  blood-slashed; her wings droop and wimple the dove.
The living dove doesn't struggle, stunned by that feral
  glory, complicit in the slow shredding toward its heart.
In the shadows under the tree, night's remaining rags
  tangle in undergrowth festooned with feathers, some
  still drifting down.
The hawk closes her switchblade talons, spreads her
  wings, and rises with the lolling, lovestruck dove.
She disappears trailing her bright cry over the trees
  bending and billowing in the rising morning wind.
Last night's rain has brought out snails, driven them on a
  leisurely stampede across the sidewalk.
There's a pomegranate tree with flowers flaming orange
  in the slanting sun, adorned with snails that have
  climbed its branches and sit along them like shiny
  brown fruit, their tentacled eyes extruded and pointed
  lightward.
I've come upon a molluscoid sacrament: the night's cold
  rain followed by the sun's warmth rendered worship-
  worthy when one lives close to the ground and the
  whole deliquescing world could melt and run at any
  moment.
And in the brightening field beyond, under the high
  grass caught between green and gold, how many
  hidden bodies?
A woodchuck dead in its burrow; the remains of a vole
  strewn by an eagle; a snake that lay basking, taken by a
  cat; or the cat itself, throat-slashed, caught in a careless
  moment by a coyote;

all the beetles, bugs, spiders, ants, slugs, and snails—
   scales, pelt, and shiny carapace—coalescing into each
   other,
stirred and strewn by rain and sun, serenaded by the
   deliberate music of the worms' subterranean ways,
   threshed and winnowed by earth's slow flail and the
   wind's soft stroke,
become soil themselves; rising in the choral heat of
   their dissolution, rising in the brightness of their
   indiscriminate, promiscuous decay, rising and rising
   in a single fluorescing chord to meet the rising sun.

All of this, being words,
may not be true.
All of this, being only words,
may not surrender
or surround
the truth,
yet it is all the truth I know
save death's silent truth,
entropy against doctrine:
only wind, sounds, words,
evaporating like breath in winter
when the endless round
of earth and stars
and the seasons' circle—
rain and snow,
frost and hard freeze
merciless summer sun
have something truer to say.

Bones In the Rain

> *Gravedigger,*
> *When you dig my grave,*
> *Could you make it shallow*
> *So that I can feel the rain,*
> *Gravedigger?*
> Dave Matthews

Myriads and multitudes of bones in the rain:
arches and rods, balls and sockets,
the hollow bones of birds,
the heavy bones of bears,
fragile sticks,
thick, keystone vertebrae,
shields of ribs,
curved and cradling pelvises—
all empty now.

Bones wake
to sunny spring showers
when rain falls like bright honey,
when the last of autumn's
cold hand hardening the earth
and winter's banked and drifted snow
reflecting moonlight in gas-blue glow are gone.

This rain eases between dirt grains
and slips through coffin lids
fills graves and vaults,
glazes bones with light,
waking them to remember
the heft and hang of flesh,
the sweet and salty taste and smell
of another's skin.

First, they long for their lost lives.
Then, the rain washes them of time,
dissolves their longing for weight,
blurs their carven names
with its infinite hammers
and tells them it's time to go.

They devise their farewells,
sung to the secret rhythms
of beetles' clatter and scrape,
the hiss of worms' passing
the twang of uncoiling fern fronds
and the whispering of windy new leaves.

They learn the joy of dissolution.
In the rain's glow
they flow to each other,
then into each other,
and in their pour they make
impossible geometries
and discover new dimensions.

They wake to the bright bliss of a single self
that escapes names and dates
carved in stone, bronze plaques
and all the gimcrack bric-a-brac
we devise just to keep them near.

After Whitman

My other self:
conspirator, emancipator whose words clear the clogged
channels of my spirit,
you touch me so the setting sun's sum fills me and,
filling, I birth this glittering evening, bending toward
night with my sight,
conspiring with the water that winks in the wind and the
sun's lengthening path on the pond and the sway of
breezy willows.
I'm drunk on the funk of harvest-turned earth and new-
cut hay and the dusky musk of last year's leaves;
I lie with you on the grassy bank where the newborn
dawn swathes and warms us, pierces us and fills us with
gentle heat, viscous and milky,
and I flood and fill with it and embrace and trace the
glitter that fills the other who opens in me, taking me
taking it in, and I swell and flow with delicious friction
and counter-friction plummeting deep and deeper;
striking fire from blooming red roses opening, where I
slowly turn, caressing their corollas and rooting deep,
wrapped in the rapture that lives in the murmurous
tides of blood in my ears;
bursting with the hot honey-ooze of this suddenly soulful
instant that fills every convolution and crenellation of
me as it lips riverbanks and floods arroyos and draws,
deepening in the light that rolls down the hills,
its uttering motion singing out in the hovering falcon,
sculling its wings in the wind to hold steady, scanning
the ground for prey then wings folded, dropping like a
spear, elongated with speed, trailing a hunting scream
like a bright dream as she takes her kill;

tranquil as the pink sow lying on her side, ear flopped
over her half-closed eye, grunting in pleasure at
the pressure of her scrabbling piglets scuffling and
snuffling at her swollen teats, filled with the poet's
ecstasy of being drained dry;
carnal as the golden odor of sun-hot balsam and sage,
the dark whiff of crushed plush geranium leaves, the
sweet smell of ripe plum and peach flesh, oozing sugar
into the air, the tender skin tight around their fibrous
gold and crimson innards,
and then all that sweet juice and tender fiber drenching
my tongue when my teeth break through;
soothed and adrift in snow's whisper on a windless
winter day, sifting through trees grown so close their
upper branches twine—oak and maple and elm and
birch and larch;
restless as the watery rush and rattle of a squall flicking
the silvery bottoms of leaves to the sky;
silent as a summer noon's stillness, its humid haze
blurring the world,
rowdy as the yellow, red, and deep brown leaves' confetti
tumbling in a cold, dry wind's clarity.
You sidle up to me from the corner of my eye when I'm
looking elsewhere;
sneak up behind me and tap my shoulder, or face me
head-on: eternal moocher, ceaseless benefactor,
playful as hide-and-no-need-to-seek.
Wait for me to catch up to you from in front where you
follow, omnivorous swallower, you and your gush of
words; impregnating source filling the present and
drowning was and will in now,
whose words, transparent, layered, bright, and
indestructible as diamond speak me and teach me how
to forgive.

Reading *Moby Dick* on the Farm, 7

And, so,
I, only, am escaped to tell thee.
Here I sit,
leaning against the indisputable trunk of this pine
with this completed book that with every word
speaks the pain of stripping illusion
and so affirms, calms, consoles
and eases the submerged life's light,
into the mind's sight
to speak from clearer sight
like the farm's necessary, severer tongue,
brother to this book.

Coda

And you,
old woman of the sea,
pale lady, sad lady
of the white eyes
and white skin
and the ashy, bitter need;
old one of my deepest sea,
eely shape-shifter;

I've met you
where I've searched you out,
waiting around every corner.
I've held you long enough.
I grant you my wish.
You are free.
Now.
Go.

Title Index

First Line Index

114